ALHA
DISNII

ALHA DISNII

My Truth

words from a
Wet'suwet'en Woman

Alha Disnii
My Truth
words from a Wet'suwet'en Woman

Copyright © 2024 Corinne George
Published in Canada by Medicine Wheel Publishing
www.medicinewheelpublishing.com

ISBN: 978-1-77854-041-7

Editor: Alicia Hibbert
Cover art painted by
Randall Tillery Fine Art
www.randaltillery.com

10   9   8   7   6   5   4   3   2   1

Printed in PRC

Funded by the   Financé par le
Government   gouvernement   Canada
of Canada   du Canada

Dedicated to my ancestors and my parents,
Gallahgun Rita and Tsaybesa Andrew George.
Also dedicated to my wonderful husband,
John, who has upheld and supported me.
For all those who respected me, treated
me with kindness, and accepted me for
who I am—you know who you are.

Contents

Sensitivity Warning

This book contains sensitive topics including—physical and sexual abuse, racism, and substance use. At times, it may be graphic in nature, with the potential to be triggering to Survivors of violence and trauma. Please be gentle with yourself, your feelings, and your truth in this process. We are holding space for you.

Foreword by
Grand Chief Stewart Phillip

*President of the Union of British
Columbia Indian Chiefs*

I am immensely grateful to know Corinne George
and am honoured to provide this foreword to
her wonderful book, *Alha disnii – My Truth*. I
met Corinne over a decade ago when she worked
at the Union of BC Indian Chiefs as a Specific
Claims Researcher, where I have been President
for twenty-five years. In addition to carrying out
her responsibilities for the UBCIC Chiefs Council
with full dedication and expertise, Corinne got to
know me and would often share her stories and
her humour with me. We remained in touch as
she moved back home to her territory, and have
marched next to each other on many occasions,
including to raise awareness about violence
against Indigenous women and girls.

Corinne's book traces her Wet'suwet'en
lineage and life story and is told with grace and
clarity. From the first sentences, she immediately draws you in and keeps you there. Her story

unfolds against the harsh backdrop of colonialism and its intersecting and multigenerational impacts, including racism and sexism. The reader has the chance to learn Corinne's story as well as the history of Canada's deeply troubled and abusive relationship with First Nations peoples, and how trauma is passed down and can be explored through a sharing of truth.

What I really enjoyed about the book was the generous opportunity that Corinne shares to get to know her and see her life. She provides a rich narrative of how her ancestors and parents guide her every day and embeds her story within an assessment of tools of resiliency they exercised, sharing how she strives to do the same. With courage and honesty, she tells her harrowing story of abuse from a very young age, how it impacted her life, and also how she was able to focus on her well-being and find love and companionship with the love of her life, John.

Corinne's book is a gift and one that is accessible. *Alha disnii – My Truth* must become educational curriculum at the school and university level, shared for broad distribution, as we strive to tell the story of colonialism, past and present.

"Reconciliation is a process of healing of relationships that requires public truth sharing, apology, and commemoration that acknowledge and redress past harms."

Truth and Reconciliation Commission, What We Have Learned: Principles of Truth and Reconciliation, p. 3

Let Me Introduce Myself

"This is my truth, and through sharing my truth, I strive for ongoing healing and to continue the journey of reconciliation. At this time of truth, it is important to remember that we need to sit with the truth for a while as we move towards Reconciliation."
—Corinne George

My name is Corinne George. I am Wet'suwet'en with Gitksan lineage[1] from the *Gidimt'en* (Bear) Clan. I was born and raised in Telkwa, BC. My parents are *Gallahgun* (Rita George)[2] and *Tsaybesa* (Andrew George Sr.). My maternal grandparents are *Naqua'ohn* (Julie Isaac) and *Satsan* (Paddy Isaac). My paternal grandparents are *Gisdaywa* (Thomas George) and *Tsaybesa* (Mary George). My great grandparents are *C'iddimsginiis* (Burns Lake Tom), *Madeek* (Bulkley Lake Isaac), *Goohlat* (Felix George), *Un'loh* (Cecilia George), and *Naqua'ohn/ Noxalay*[3] (Christine Patsy-Tom), all of whom are Wet'suwet'en and/or Gitksan Hereditary Chiefs. It is important to note that some of my ancestors were also elected leaders. Felix George was the first Chief of *Tse Kya*,[4] and Paddy Isaac was elected Chief of the Burns Lake Band.

My ancestors guide me as I strive for a strong connection to my culture and identity despite the impacts of colonization. Through the last few years, I started to recognize more fully the traumas of colonization for my ancestors, but I have also begun to acknowledge and speak about my personal and historical trauma. This is my truth,[5] and through sharing my truth, I strive for ongoing healing and to continue the journey of reconciliation. Despite various challenges, I embraced my identity as a Wet'suwet'en woman and maintained a strong connection to my culture.

1

My Great Grandparents, My Grandparents, and My Parents

—

" As a result of land ownership, my grandparents and their offspring, including my father, were enfranchised, meaning they no longer had their 'Indian Status.' When my mother married my father, she lost her status and was no longer allowed to reside on-reserve. "

My great grandparents, grandparents, and parents influence and guide me every single day of my life. They all upheld their cultures and traditions and passed their knowledge to the ensuing generations. Living off *Niwh Yintah* (our territories), fully participating in our *Balhats* (Feast system), and engaging the hereditary system were foundational as they navigated through the ever-changing world when settlers arrived in Wet'suwet'en territory. Trauma and colonization, racism, and an increasingly shifting reality were reasons to rely more heavily on our culture and traditions and move forward in the best possible ways. The tools of resiliency by way of walking well in both worlds were passed on from generation to generation. I strive to embrace those tools and follow the trails blazed by my ancestors to the best of my ability.

My great grandparents are *C'iddimsginiis* (Burns Lake Tom) and *Naqua'ohn/Noxalay* (Christine Patsy Tom); *Madeek* (Bulkley Lake

Isaac) and Agnes Augusta; *Goohlat* (Felix George) and *Un'loh* (Cecilia George); and James Wells and Cecilia Jenny. Although I did not meet my great grandparents, their legacy and their ways continue to influence me every day. My oral history tells me that my great grandparents were leaders. They were Wet'suwet'en Hereditary Chiefs; in my maternal lineage, they were Wet'suwet'en as well as Gitksan Hereditary Chiefs. As previously mentioned, some of my ancestors were also highly respected elected leaders. Figure 1 on page 56 shows my great grandfather *Goohlat* (Felix George) on the right side of the photo, giving a speech at the opening of the Hagwilget *(Tse Kya)* Bridge in both his capacity as Hereditary Chief as well as an elected leader. He bridged cultures while still embracing traditional and cultural values. Much like today, I am certain that navigating the reality between our ancestral ways that might need to shift in reaction to changing contemporary circumstances was an incredible challenge. From what I understand, my great grandmother *Un'loh* (Cecilia George) walked with my great grandfather in the realms of traditional and cultural ways. My great grandfather Felix had influence and connection to the land from the south side of Francois Lake to *Bi winii* (Owen Lake) and through to *Tse Kya*.

My maternal great grandparents are *C'iddimsginiis* (Burns Lake Tom) and *Naqua'ohn/ Noxalay* (Christine Patsy Tom); and *Madeek* (Bulkley Lake Isaac) and Agnes Augusta. My great grandmother Christine's marriage to Burns Lake Tom was her second marriage. It was during this marriage that she gave birth to my grandmother Julie; my grandmother had seven sisters and one brother. My mother, through her sharing of oral history, told me that it was *C'iddimsginiis* Burns Lake Tom who cleared the land on which Burns Lake, BC, is now situated. I stand by this truth. My mother shared with me that my great grandfather Burns Lake Tom ran a trap line on the creek that we know as *Tsilh Kaz Kwah* that runs through the center of the Village of Burns Lake. He dropped an axe in the creek, and the axe floated down the creek towards the lake. This is where the name *Tsilh Kaz Kwah* comes from. I proudly acknowledge this truth of my ancestors.

My great grandfather *Madeek* (Bulkley Lake Isaac) resided on the shores of Bulkley Lake. His mother lived only about ½ kilometre from *C'iggiz*.[6] I don't know very much about my great-great grandmother except she resided on the

9

shores of "Old Woman Lake" and that is where the English name derives from. My mother said that my great-great grandmother used to sit by the lake and smoke a pipe. Someone set fire to my great grandfather's cabin at Bulkley Lake, and he was burned off his land. My mother explained that the Indian Agent at the time did not assist my great grandfather in any way except to provide some ointment for his wife's foot, which was badly burned. My grandfather was then provided with a piece of land in lieu of his cabin at Bulkley Lake, which is where my grandparents and my mother's family have resided since that time. This is called *C'iggiz*, where my mother was born and raised and where our family continues to reside.

My maternal grandparents were *Satsan* (Paddy Isaac) and *Naqua'ohn* (Julie Isaac). My grandfather Paddy held the Hereditary Chief name *Satsan* from the *Gilseryhu* (Caribou/Small Frog) Clan. I have been told that my grandfather Paddy was a traditional man who provided for his family from the land and who also owned and operated a railway tie camp behind *C'iggiz* throughout the 1940s and 50s. The tie camp employed both Aboriginal and non-Aboriginal people from all over the region. My grandpa Paddy's ability to hold strong to Wet'suwet'en culture and tradition while navigating the contemporary economy was very evident. Sadly, he was killed while walking on the highway near *C'iggiz* in 1960, eleven years before I was born, so I did not meet him.

My grandmother, *Naqua'ohn* (Julie Isaac) of the *Gidimt'en,* passed away when I was five years old. Her strength, beauty, and grace flow through our family—her influence remains strong with me. I remember her as petite, shy, and gentle. She always wore floral dresses, had her hair pinned back, and wore knitted slippers with pom-poms. We visited her whenever possible as I was growing up. My grandmother and grandfather are shown in figure 2 on page 57 in front of *C'iggiz* (Duncan Lake).

My paternal grandparents were *Gisdaywa* (Thomas George) from the *Gidimt'en* Clan and *Tsaybesa* (Mary George) from the *Likhts'amisyu* Clan (Killer Whale clan). My siblings, my cousins, and I affectionately referred to them as "Mama and Papa." We were all raised at *Toh Tsiw'diini* (which we called "Toody-Ni"). Our grandparents resided on pre-empted[7] land that one of my grandmother's relations provided for the family. As a result of land ownership, my grandparents and their offspring, including my father, were enfranchised, meaning they no longer had their

11

"Indian Status." My aunts and uncles and my father all received parcels of land at *Toody-Ni* and were also considered "non-status Indians."

Toody-Ni was home and Mama and Papa were central for us. As their descendants, we grew up closely, and instead of first cousins, in many ways we were like siblings. We all played together and gathered at Mama and Papa's house. We spent so much time playing outside and by the river. We were free in so many respects. Our playground extended from the hill loaded with juniper to the river full of fish. In the summer, we fished, picked berries, and played outside, and in the winter months, we skated, tobogganed, and gathered at Mama and Papa's place around the woodstove to warm our bodies, hearts, and spirits. We drank tea and ate pilot biscuits with Mama, listening to her share her stories and sat with her as she made moccasins or buckskin coats. Living in our ancestral ways while selling items she made of moose hide was one of her ways to navigate both Wet'suwet'en and Western economies.

Growing up in *Toody-Ni* was deeply foundational—our parents and grandparents taught us the ways of the Wet'suwet'en. We were also shown the value of learning contemporary realities. For example, Mama and Papa were both entrepreneurs as my grandfather sold furs from trapping, which was quite lucrative, and my grandmother made and sold moccasins, leather gloves, and buckskin jackets. Both my grandparents were highly respected Wet'suwet'en Hereditary Chiefs who were active in the *Balhats* system; they were traditional but also had to adapt to a certain degree to the Western economy. My grandfather travelled the grease trails. The grease trails were a network of trails for trading ancestral foods—named after eulichan grease, which was one of the trade commodities. My ancestors would trade items such as moose and berries for seafood items with our western Aboriginal neighbours. Papa also travelled with a pack horse when starting work with the Grand Trunk Pacific Railway. If I were to use one word to describe Papa, it would be "humble." He passed away when I was three years old, and I have one snapshot memory of him. My mother brought me to visit Mama and Papa, and I remember Papa bending down, shaking my hand, and saying *"Haddit! Soh'enzin'!?"* which means "Hello! How are you!?" in Wet'suwet'en. His eyes sparkled, and his smile was wide and joyful. Mama and Papa continue to influence me every day. Figures 3 and 4 on pages 58 and 59 are photos of *Gisdaywa* and *Tsaybesa* with their regalia, as well as their respective totem poles. Respect. Honour. Truth. Love. Culture. And Hope.

Mama and Papa were traditional and also open-minded. They were very strong in the Wet'suwet'en *Balhats* system and were deeply connected to *Niwh Yintah*; when the economy shifted, they navigated the shift, retaining a strong connection to their culture and identity. While holding strong to Wet'suwet'en cultures and traditions, they also accepted and embraced Catholicism or Western Christianity, for example. From what I remember and from what my mother continues to share through oral history, they embraced the "good" from so many circumstances and forged their own paths. In essence, they embraced universal values of goodness, peace, and light. I absolutely love to sing "Carrier Hymns" for this reason. Carrier[8] Hymns arose from our historical connection to Catholicism. I always witnessed my ancestors singing the hymns and saw them as beautiful and peaceful. I sing these hymns today as they remain a strong connection to my ancestors. Mama and Papa were very humble, traditional, faithful, and forward thinking. Maintaining a strong connection to our cultural values while

navigating contemporary and Western economies was critical for our survival.

My mother, *Gallahgun* (Rita George), and
father, *Tsaybesa* (Andrew George Sr.), provided
me and my siblings with a solid cultural and
historical foundation based on the *Yintah*
(Wet'suwet'en ancestral territory). Mom and
dad got married in 1960. Dad was twenty years
older than my mom. Together, they had seven
children, one of which was a miscarriage. As
children, we spent so much time on *Niwh Yintah*
on our matrilineal clan territory (*Gidimt'en*)
and my father's clan territory (*Likhts'amisyu*).
Our food staples were from the land: salmon,
fish (trout), moose meat, beaver meat, grouse,
rabbit, huckleberries, as well as various other
berries. My father was also a trapper who sold
furs for income to help provide for our family.
Our time on the land was life-giving in so many
ways. Through passing down their knowledge of
Wet'suwet'en culture and history and providing
for us with food from the land, our parents
amplified their roles as life-givers.

My mother has always been very traditional
in the ways of the Wet'suwet'en. Throughout her
childhood, she worked alongside her parents as
they hunted, gathered, and trapped. Much of her
time was spent on *Niwh Yintah*, and she passed

on so much of her knowledge to her children. During my mother's childhood, she spent a lot of time learning from the elders. Her knowledge of territories, genealogy, our language, and various cultures and traditions is vast and deep.

As a young girl, my mother attended Lejac Indian Residential School just outside of Fraser Lake, BC. She attended the school for four years. She remembers the strict and regimented ways of the residential school and explained that she spent much of her time cooking and cleaning. Although my mother shared that she did not directly experience abuse at residential school, she witnessed severe mistreatment of her peers, particularly after they attempted to run away, back to their homes. She recalled in one circumstance that after some of the children ran away, they were brought back, and at mealtime they had to line up by the other children, and they were whipped in front of everyone. She said that to this day, she can still hear the sharp sound of the whips. While my mother did not directly experience abuse, her memories of Lejac include strict discipline, regimented schedules, sadness, and fear. She also acknowledges that so many children experienced incredible levels of trauma and pain at residential schools. As a young girl, I remember my mother sharing with me stories of

her time at residential school and remarking to
her: "That sounds like a prison!"

Although my mother retained the
Wet'suwet'en language and remains a fluent
speaker, she recalled that during her time at
Lejac, she was forbidden to speak Wet'suwet'en.
She remembered that many were punished when
attempting to speak their own languages. Later
in her life, when she had her own children, she
decided that it was more important that her
children learn to speak English. This is one of
the reasons why my siblings and I did not learn
fluent Wet'suwet'en.

My mother was groomed to take on
her role by the ancestors, including and
especially my grandfather, *Gisdaywa* (Thomas
George). She shared with me how several
Wet'suwet'en Hereditary Chiefs visited with
my grandfather, and collectively they decided
that my mother would take on a Hereditary
Chief name—*Gallahgun*. My mother spoke of
how Papa ensured that both she and my father
raised their children on *Niwh Yintah* and in the
Balhats. My mother and father made sure that
we participated in the *Balhats* from a very young
age. I have memories of falling asleep under my
mother's chair at the *Balhats*, and then, as I grew
older, I sat in front of mom. In the Wet'suwet'en

Balhats, the *Denize* (male Chiefs) and *Tsakize* (female Chiefs) sat in the back row, and the *Skiyze* (future Chiefs or children of Chiefs) sat in the front rows. My mother always asked that I remain seated and watch and listen: "Don't run around. Sit down and listen!" It wasn't until later in life that I understood the importance of this as I fondly reminisce about so many of our ancestors in the *Balhats*. I remember watching the business take place in the Feast Hall, and I remember all of our ancestors who have since passed on. Although I did not know how to speak Wet'suwet'en, I understood that I was witnessing my culture in action. My mother had explained to me the true meaning of the term *Deni n'aas,* which is often used interchangeably with the term *Balhats* or Feast. She explained that when the host clan seats Hereditary Chiefs upon entry to the *Balhats* hall while holding a talking stick, leading the Chief to their seat, the Chief being seated "walks with dignity." Thus, the literal meaning is: "to walk with dignity." This memory of my ancestors remains strong within me. I remember witnessing the old peo-ple walk into the *Balhats* hall with tremendous dignity. This is also an example of the types of oral history that my mother has shared with me.

The Wet'suwet'en are a matrilineal culture; thus, because my matriarchs are *Gidimt'en* (Bear Clan), I am *Gidimt'en*, as are all of my siblings. Our matriarchs are central and we learn from our matriarchs. I continue to learn on a daily basis from my mother, who has incredible oral history and lived experiences.

My father was a trapper, hunter, Wet'suwet'en Hereditary Chief, and he was also a proud veteran of the Second World War. He spent most of his life on *Niwh Yintah*, and as a result, his knowledge of Wet'suwet'en ancestral territories was vast. As a young man, my father continued to spend all his time on *Niwh Yintah,* however when WWII started, he went for basic training and eventually went overseas as a soldier. Dad spent about four years overseas. He was in the 2nd Canadian Field Company of the Royal Canadian Engineers and earned the rank of Sapper. Among his various duties, he assisted in dismantling land mines and building bailey bridges. Dad was also an accomplished carpenter and often spoke of the projects he was part of in terms of "building bridges" upon his return home. I carried his analogy as a bridge builder —for me, it is about building bridges between cultures. This is a legacy that I strive for by following my father's example. My father shared so many stories about his time as a soldier. He spoke of his extreme experiences and all that he witnessed while overseas. Upon return, his parents exclaimed: "A return soldier!" They very much understood his reason for going to war and also they understood his sacrifice. His experience as a young soldier forever changed his worldview and his life. While he returned as a veteran who fought for the freedom of Canada, he was also rejected in so many ways. For example, he often spoke of how badly mistreated and disrespected he was as an "Indian" even though he sacrificed his life for those in our collective society. Colonial systems were not kind to returning soldiers as, in the eyes of so many, despite their enfranchisement, they were viewed as "Indians" and forbidden to enter certain establishments. Aboriginal veterans were so deeply disrespected despite their contributions to the war efforts.

Both my father and my mother taught us the importance of our seasonal rounds to survive. Seasonal rounds are the ways in which the ancestors harvested, hunted, and gathered, which aligned with the seasons. Everything the Wet'suwet'en ate and used was done in accordance with the seasons; knowledge was passed on from generation to generation.

When my mother married my father, she lost her status and was no longer allowed to reside on-reserve, and as a result, all their children also did not have status (see figure 6 on page 61). My mother speaks with so much grief when she reflects on her move away from her family and to Telkwa. She was very limited in her ability to visit with family as she was told that she was no longer able to visit the reserve. She wept often as she missed her mother, her family, and her home so much. We were raised as non-status Indians (we were not recognized as an "Indian" under the Indian Act). It wasn't until 1985, when this part of the Indian Act was amended under Bill C-31, that we were recognized as "Indian." Upon marriage, they moved to *Toody-Ni*, where my grandparents granted them a five-acre parcel of land. This became our home for many years.

Both my parents received little formal Western education, however with their combined training on *Niwh Yintah* and knowledge of our traditions, they provided for the family in the best possible ways. My father worked at the Smithers Indian Friendship Centre,[9] and my mother worked at the tree nursery. Their combined income was often not enough for us to survive in the Western economy, so we relied heavily on traditional food from the territory.

Somehow, my mother always managed to put food on the table for us, no matter what. There were times, however, when I was unable to bring a lunch to school and I remember telling the teachers that I either forgot my lunch at home or that I lost it. It was not uncommon that the teacher would ask other students if they had items that they would be able to share with me. It was rare that we ate chicken, pork chops, or beef. Our staples were salmon and moose meat. My beautiful mother amazed me with her ability to make sure there was supper every day. The fact that the Western economy took such a toll on our family was not my mother's or my father's fault. They did everything they could to make sure we did not starve.

My mother was also a translator for the landmark *Delgamuukw/Gisdaywa* case in which the Gitksan and Wet'suwet'en Hereditary Chiefs claimed ownership and jurisdiction over our traditional territories (and were eventually victorious). This was a strongly pivotal moment for our nations. She translated the plaintiffs' knowledge from Wet'suwet'en to English and vice versa. My mother's knowledge of Wet'suwet'en culture and tradition is not only from her own experiences but also from hearing the oral histories first-hand. She fondly remembers spending time with all the Hereditary Chiefs, who were her elders at the time, and hearing the history of the Wet'suwet'en from them. Mom said that her involvement as a translator was her way of protecting the territories. My father was also very instrumental in the court case. His knowledge of the territories was so strong. He supported the Hereditary Chiefs and all involved in the case. When mom and dad took us out on *Niwh Yintah*, both of them often shared their oral histories and knowledge of territories and the boundaries.

Despite their best attempts, there were times when the Western economy got the best of our family. We struggled financially and the impact of Western values had a deep effect on us. My father confronted the impacts of the war, and both my father and mother faced the impacts of colonization. When dad passed away in 1998, mom and dad had just celebrated thirty-eight years of marriage; they had a resilient marriage with moments of hardship and conflict. There was so much joy as well, particularly when we spent time on *Niwh Yintah*, and they did their best to make sure we strived for success. They guided us to keep one foot in our traditions while striving for success in the Western world; thus, the best of both worlds. Celebrations for positive moments and successes were also very much present in our lives. While they shared their traditional knowledge with us, they encouraged us to excel in all areas of our lives. So, when we graduated from high school and on to college or university, they celebrated our success through sharing the achievements with everyone. They were very proud!

My mother and father have always been deeply in touch with our culture, and they carried the oral history and oral traditions of our ancestors with beautiful strength, integrity, and grace. My father was a hunter and trapper, my mother was a gatherer and hunter, and both were Hereditary Chiefs who worked together in the ways of our ancestors. My parents are my heroes.

2

My Childhood

—

" *Our family income, combined with traditional food, sustained us for the most part as my mother and father did all they could to provide for their six children. There were, however, times when we had little in our fridge, and we were hungry. That was neither Mom nor Dad's fault, as the Western economy catered to those with Western education.* "

Born and raised in *Toody-Ni,* I was the youngest of the generation of "the Georges," the grandchildren of Thomas and Mary George —Mama and Papa. My fondest and most important memories include walking *Niwh Yintah* with my mom, dad, and siblings. My earliest and most important memories include walking from my mother's clan territory to my father's clan territory. I was so small that I had to be carried across the creeks. We spent days walking on the trails of our ancestors. Mom and dad made sure that we became very familiar with *Niwh Yintah.*

My father shot moose, and as a family, we harvested the moose. When we got back home, we always watched mom and assisted as she butchered the moose. Most of the time, my Uncle Roy (my mother's cousin) would provide salmon for our family, and for that, we are forever grateful; after mom worked on the salmon or moose, we would watch and help mom freeze, jar, or smoke the moose and salmon for our winter food supply. Whenever possible, our family feasted on grouse or rabbit. My brother snared rabbits, and often, I would walk with him as he walked the trails. Watching dad on the territories and watching mom work on our food supply was magic and these are among my absolute favourite memories.

I also remember, as a young girl, helping pick potatoes with our family to supplement the family income. Our family income, combined with traditional food, sustained us for the most part as my mother and father did all they could to provide for their six children. There were, however, times when we had little in our fridge, and we were hungry. That was neither mom nor dad's fault, as the Western economy catered to those with Western education. The harsh reality was that we were often hungry. But one of my other favourite memories includes my father and my mother making me some hot chocolate and my father making us oatmeal, which we referred to as "mush."

Prior to going to preschool, I stayed with Mama during the day while mom and dad went to work. Mom and dad picked me up after work to go home for supper. I used to sit and drink tea and eat pilot biscuits with Mama as early as the age of four. I watched her work with leather and prepare traditional food for lunch. It was during one of these times when a visitor showed up at my grandmother's place, took me upstairs, and sexually abused me. I was four or five years old at the time (before Kindergarten). At the time, I had no idea what was happening, and I did not tell anyone. I really don't know how often this occurred, but I know that it happened more than once. During one of those times, I remember my grandma and my aunt coming upstairs. I don't remember much of what happened after that, but I think that was the last time that occurred. I never told anyone about those occurrences for many, many years. This was not an isolated incident, as sexual abuse occurred on at least one other occasion when I was a young girl. As I got older, I did not realize it at the time, but the level of severity of the abuse affected my social interactions. This fact, in addition to being an Aboriginal child in a primarily non-Aboriginal village and school, greatly affected my ability to fit in and be accepted. I experienced trauma on various levels by the time I reached elementary school.

Having been raised off-reserve in Telkwa and Smithers, I was among the few Aboriginal students in the preschool, elementary, and high school settings. Not knowing at the time how "different I was," I always strived to do the best I could, whether it was in schoolwork, sports, or other activities. I had some wonderful friends through my school years. While many accepted me for who I was (and I am so grateful for that!), there were also so many to whom I was invisible or those who did not acknowledge my existence as a human being. There were moments when I had strong feelings that others viewed me as dirty and ugly. In extreme circumstances, I was beaten, and in other situations, I was called a "stupid squaw!!" These early and formative experiences had adverse impacts on my overall well-being.

As I left preschool and entered grade one, my parents made the decision to move me to St. Joseph's Catholic School in Smithers. Their intent was to make sure that I would be able to receive my first communion. While there, my social skills remained on a different level due to my early experiences of abuse and, at the same time, I had moved into a school in which there was an equal number of Aboriginal students and non-Aboriginal students. This would also be one of the first times I was directly affected by systemic violence.

One of the school rules at the Catholic School was "do not go on the steps at recess or lunch" as we were to play on the playground. Being new to the school, I was not aware of some of the rules. During one recess, one of the children on the playground got badly hurt and had a bleeding nose. I was very curious and followed the child to the steps of the school when one of the recess supervisors escorted the child inside. I looked in the window by the entrance to see how the other students were, and there were a few others who were just as curious as I was. Suddenly, one of the school staff members came outside onto the steps and told those of us on the steps to go to the principal's office. There were about four of us who were escorted into the principal's office. They brought a couple of the other students into the office, and suddenly, I heard some slapping and bursts of crying. I had no idea what was happening. I was asked to come forward into the office. When I entered the office, the principal asked me to hold out my hand. When I held out my hand, Sister Margaret extended her arm outstretched in the air, and I felt a sharp pain rush up my arm and throughout my body. She raised her arm again and struck my open hand with a wooden ruler. I don't remember how many times she did this, but I am certain that it was at least four or five times. I screamed in pain, and although I tried hard not to react, I started to yell and cry. To this day, I don't know what I did that was so terribly wrong that I deserved a beating with a wooden ruler—other than the fact that I went on the steps at recess.

It is very important to note that there were many kind-hearted and wonderful friends throughout my childhood. There were some who treated me as an equal and accepted me as a friend. They made such a tremendous difference in my life. Further, there were some teachers who made a deep impact on me. For example, one of my elementary teachers used to give individually wrapped candies as a prize for perfect assignments. This teacher also put a poem on display every Monday, and by each Friday, we were given an opportunity to recite the poem by memory. For each stanza we remembered, we were given one individually wrapped candy. For a little girl who did not have the opportunity to enjoy a lot of sweets, this was a great incentive. This moment in my childhood helped me form study habits and memorization, things that would help me later in life. I am incredibly grateful for those who accepted me and deeply influenced my life in a good way. For the most part, I tried to excel in school and in sports and fit in with my peers. I played softball, joined the trampoline club, ran in track and field, and played soccer. Often, I did not "fit in," but I still engaged in physical activity and played on teams in an attempt to fit in and to try to do well.

When I was elementary school age, several instances occurred within my family that presented incredible challenges. There were many tragic deaths in our extended family that deeply affected both sides of our family. While I do not wish to disclose details of all that occurred (out of respect for the immediate families), I will speak to one death that affected me. My cousin, who was at the time a young Aboriginal woman, went missing. I remember travelling with the older members of our family who were searching for her. I did not know what to expect had we found her, so I was very much on edge. This experience might have occurred when I was about seven or eight years old. As I reflect on this experience, I remember feeling the hurt and the pain of my family who were searching for her. I remember overhearing the older members of our family discuss speculations about what they thought might have happened to her. Even at a very young age, I was aware of the extreme nature of this circumstance and understood what had happened. This memory and other experiences like this remained with me throughout my life. Her remains were found a while after she disappeared. Her death remains unsolved to this day. This experience is, in part, why the issue of Missing and Murdered Indigenous Women is so near and dear to my heart; I have had family members and friends deeply traumatized by this extremely painful reality.

While my mother and father were central to my life, as were (and still are) my siblings, other positive influences remained prominent. *Niwh Yintah* and the *Balhats,* as well as all other ancestral teachings, were foundational; we continued to rely on the territory for our livelihood. Spending time on the territory with my mom, dad, and siblings is among my most treasured memories. Although one of the most traumatic and life-altering abuses occurred at my grandma's home, it is also ironic that visiting with Mama (I was only three when Papa passed away) was one of the more positive influences in my life. Watching Mama work with leather and listening to her stories while the woodstove burned has always been a soothing memory for me. Even though I was a little girl, I enjoyed drinking tea with her. She had a catechism Bible from 1913 and she used to sit with me and show me the pictures and tell me stories of the Bible. To this day, I remember her leathery fingers pointing at the pictures and sharing the stories.

When Mama passed away in 1981, my dad, aunts, and uncles called me to her place when they were going through her belongings. They told me that they knew how much Mama loved me and that they wanted to give me the 1913 Catechism Bible. I continue to cherish that Bible to this day.

Although I have certainly had some unfortunate and hurtful experiences, my personal relationship with the Catholic Church has had a positive influence on me. I fully understand and acknowledge the multiple levels of pain and trauma endured by so many. As I pointed out earlier, I have also been hurt and traumatized by those in the Church. At the same time, I will speak to other ways the Church influenced me. I was only nine years old when I received the "Sacrament of Confirmation" in the Catholic Church in Telkwa. Bishop Fergus O'Grady visited the church to administer the confirmation. At one point, as part of the ceremony, I kneeled in front of him during the service and in front of the congregation, he wrapped his hands gently around mine and said: "My hands are cold! Maybe you can help warm them up!" and he giggled joyfully. I felt very safe with him as his eyes danced and his laugh was joyful. After mass, he spent time with me amid the busyness of the congregation. We talked, and he asked me so many questions about who I am and my schooling. When leaving, he gave me his mailing address and asked me to write to him and that he would write back. I started to write letters to him, and he always wrote back. We wrote back and forth until well after I graduated from high school. Bishop O'Grady was kind, compassionate, and caring, and he always acknowledged and respected me. Here is an excerpt from one of his letters:

Congratulations on your high mark in your math test and in now being in grade six. You will soon be in High School.

I hope you ran in the "Terry Fox Run." Here at the College our boys and girls got the trophy for having the largest number in the run.

Tell your dad I will continue to pray for him.

At that time, my father was not well, so I appreciated his kind thoughts. I kept several letters and gifts that Bishop O'Grady sent to me. These were great reminders of his support and encouragement to me as I grew up. Again, I fully understand and acknowledge that Bishop O'Grady had a very contentious role in the oppression and historical relationship with the Aboriginal community. That said, his relationship with me was foundational because of his kindness and personal relationship with me as an individual. During one of our many visits, he remarked to me how he enjoyed receiving my letters: "You are a good writer. You write as though you are speaking…" This moment of acknowledgement spoke to me and gave me confidence in my writing.

When I became a teenager and left elementary school, the divide between me and many of my peers widened. While I tended to get into more trouble, I struggled with the desire to fit in and to try to do well in school amidst racial tension. Again, as a young Aboriginal girl surviving in a non-Aboriginal environment, there were often serious challenges. Often, I was rejected, laughed at, scorned, or alienated. For example, no matter how hard I excelled in school and joined sports teams or other clubs, I was often alienated and not "part of the group." I attempted to excel in Basketball and Track and Field. I am so grateful for those who accepted me and respected me.

As I grew older and entered middle school and high school, the gap between me and many of my "peers" increased. While so many moved onto the popular circles, to many I became increasingly invisible. As a result, I did all that I could to attract attention, including getting into trouble—quite often. My social skills were lacking, and throughout my high school years, there were many to whom I was invisible and those who did not acknowledge my existence as a human being. I was marginalized and overlooked. I often felt "less than" or was outwardly scorned.

But my social network did expand in high school while I navigated the social structures within a non-Aboriginal setting. I continued to strive for success in the realms of schoolwork, sports, and social interactions. Due to financial constraints, I was unable to join track and field, but the basketball coaches came up with ways to make basketball affordable for prospective team members, and I was able to join basketball. Despite some of the dynamics, I still managed to excel and became one of the more valuable players on the team. While my social network expanded, I enjoyed the comfort of some wonderful friends. In other activities like student council, writing for the school newspaper and participating in clubs, things had started to shift, and more people became accepting of me, and many teachers were very encouraging and supportive. Many of those teachers influenced me through my life journey. One of the more formative experiences included an opportunity to write for the school newspaper. I really enjoyed the opportunity and found a passion for writing. I am so incredibly grateful for the teachers who encouraged me and supported me. One day, I was getting ready to complete an assignment, and one of my teachers said to me: "Oh ... nobody ever gets an 'A' on this assignment in my class ... " Of course, I worked very hard on that assignment and polished it. I submitted the assignment. I got an "A." Later on, I realized that he guided me to that outcome. This experience was one moment of many that sparked me to excel further.

When I was in grade nine, the landmark *Delgamuukw/Gisdaywa* court case trial started. Gitksan and Wet'suwet'en Hereditary Chiefs claimed ownership and jurisdiction of our respective ancestral territories. So many of my family members were deeply involved in the case, and my ancestors' words and experiences were foundational in the oral histories and oral traditions connected to the case. I started to attend the trial hearings after school every day. During one of those days, as I sat in the hearings, I heard Judge Allen McEachern state that oral history was hearsay. I leaned over to the person beside me and asked: "What is hearsay?" Upon hearing the definition, I was immediately appalled as I could not believe that our oral histories and traditions were so deeply disrespected. Even though I was shocked by this, I need to admit that there were many times that I lost my way, not always knowing how to honour traditions and basically being a young person who was apt to make mistakes. I said things and did things that did not align with my ancestral ways. Later in life, that would be an important lesson as to why it takes our Hereditary Chiefs many, many years of grooming.

The *Delgamuukw/Gisdaywa* court case was extremely significant. At the same time, because of the nature of the "land claim" label, racial tensions started to flare in the Bulkley Valley. Being one of the few Aboriginal students at the high school, I found myself having to confront racist remarks. The racist remarks not only occurred in the school but also in the community. I started to become more outspoken, and even though, at times, I was engulfed in confusion, I also tried to navigate my way beyond the racial tension. As a result of my involvement in more political movements, I became involved as a "non-status Indian" in the United Native Nations. As a young person, one of my mentors at the time thought I had some potential and paved the way for me to attend the first-ever National Aboriginal Youth Conference in Ottawa hosted by the Native Council of Canada. Yet again, someone acknowledged me and also upheld my desire to be heard. Shortly after that, I was invited to an Aboriginal Education symposium in Montreal. While at both events, I was inspired to see so many strong and confident youth and up-and-coming leaders. In addition, while in Ottawa, Jim Fulton from the New Democratic Party who was the Member of Parliament for Skeena-Bulkley Valley, had invited me for lunch. It was quite a thrill for this young Wet'suwet'en girl from Smithers to enjoy lunch on Parliament Hill. All of these experiences had a profound impact on me as they were moments of acknowledgement.

The National Aboriginal Youth Conference in Ottawa was such a memorable and amazing experience for me. I was only fifteen at the time, and I remember meeting so many inspiring Aboriginal youth. I was absolutely fascinated by their confidence, determination, and intelligence. All those in attendance inspired me to be proud of my identity and my background. Through the years, I witnessed so many of them achieve so many great successes. I will always remember that experience as powerful and inspirational.

As I navigated high school, I strived for my best. Without a doubt in my mind, I fell short. I made so many mistakes as some of my social skills were deeply affected by earlier experiences, and I also acted out. I started to drink alcohol, and although I managed to keep my head above water in that realm, I still struggled. One of the activities that helped me stay balanced was my relationship with the Catholic Church and Bishop O'Grady. My relationship with the Church was certainly not without its challenges, as racial dynamics were also evident in the confines of the institution. But I managed to cling to the goodness. I used to attend a Catholic Camp just outside of Fort St. James called Camp Morice. Many there accepted me, and in particular, Bishop O'Grady's influence was strong. I very much looked forward to spending time with some of my friends and visiting with Bishop O'Grady. It was moments like this that gave me life and kept me balanced. The dynamic of being "less than" due to moments of racial tensions was a reality even at Camp Morice; however, I still fondly reflect on much of my time there.

I struggled and yet survived my childhood and teen years in Telkwa and Smithers. I graduated from Smithers Senior Secondary in 1989. I enjoyed the graduation with my friends and tried to overcome the fact that, for so many, I remained invisible through all the school years. These dynamics, along with disrespectful treatment, would become one of my trauma triggers (due to intense racism and alienation) for me later in life.

Throughout all my years of schooling, I always gravitated towards social studies/history or physical education. Thus, upon graduating from high school, I had my sights set on becoming a history and physical education high school teacher. I was accepted to Capilano College, and I was determined to succeed. Within a month of graduating from high school, I was off to the big city to attend college.

3

A Dark Trail—Off the Trails of My Ancestors

—

So many times, I am certain that I came so close to death. Marks, bruises, and black eyes were common for me. Whenever this occurred, I stayed away from family and friends until the marks went away...The beatings lasted for years, and I did everything I could to try to leave, only to end up in the relationship again.

When I got to Vancouver to go to college, I was immediately drawn to the hustle and bustle of the city. I was only eighteen at the time, and therefore, I felt ready for adventure. I had the summer ahead of me before starting my first semester at Capilano College in North Vancouver. I am so fortunate to have had one of my siblings welcome me to stay with him in Mount Pleasant in East Vancouver. I secured a job working at a tourist destination for a little over five dollars an hour. In alignment with striving to keep in balance, I joined a slow-pitch team, given my passion for sports. Everything was wonderful and full of promise as I was learning how to survive in the city.

During the summer in Vancouver, I spent a lot of time playing ball, but at the same time, the party lifestyle became more attractive to me. I started to make awful choices and became exposed to the darker side of the party lifestyle. Don't get me wrong, there were certainly some fun people with whom I spent time, but for the most part, I slid into an abyss. To make matters worse, I met a man who was fourteen years my senior who paid attention to me. I was very naïve and young at the time, so I reacted to his attention towards me and ended up in a relationship with him. At first, it seemed wonderful that an older, good-looking non-Aboriginal man would express any interest in me (as an Aboriginal girl growing up in Telkwa and Smithers, it was very rare that interracial relationships existed). I started to lose sight of the trails of my ancestors and followed a dark trail. The trail of darkness extended from the time I was eighteen until the time I was about twenty-three. A short time, but with long-standing impacts.

When I started school at Capilano College, my values and my focus turned towards my relationship (which by this time had reached well past the toxic level) and towards alcohol. My grades started to suffer and I made a shift to attend Langara College, which was closer to my home in East Vancouver. My life, my decisions, and my lifestyle continued to spiral, but I still managed to transfer to Langara College. It was during this time that my "relationship" took a turn for the worse, and I started to get physically beaten. I continued school, and the beatings became more severe, and I started to rely more heavily on alcohol to numb the pain. Things spiralled, and the abuse turned into not only physical abuse but emotional, spiritual, mental, and verbal abuse: "You fat, ugly squaw!" or "You stupid, ugly squaw!!" were yelled in my ears during the beatings. At this time, I averaged about 115 pounds and was still fairly athletic. In between the beatings, he always made comments about me needing to lose more weight. So, I did—an attempt to try to gain his acceptance.

So many times I am certain that I came close to death. Marks, bruises, and black eyes were common for me. Whenever this occurred, I stayed away from family and friends until the marks went away. On a few occasions, some saw my bruises and were suspicious and did not believe that I "ran into a door" or that I "fell." One time, I was slapped so hard that my cheeks had hand imprints on them. But this was risky for him, so he started to beat me in ways that the bruises would not show. For example, one time he banged my head very hard against the floor several times. The next day, there weren't any visible signs of physical abuse, but I had at least five or six very serious welts on the back of my head. I tried to fight back to defend myself, I yelled, I name-called, I said and did things that were awful, and it just became a violent and vicious cycle. I became a person that I did not want to be. The beatings lasted for years, and I did everything I could to try to leave, only to end up in the relationship again. I spent some time in transition homes, and I often wonder what might have happened to me had I not had such a critically important resource. In addition to being caught up in a vicious cycle, I came to a realization much later in life that one of the other subconscious reasons I kept returning to that relationship was an attempt to gain control over that area in my life.

During my young adult years, I lost so much of myself, and I started to lose my spirit. I drank to numb the pain, and while I was out there on the "social scene," I faced abuse in various forms. Sexual assault occurred several times, even with those I trusted. I no longer knew who I had become. The toll of the trauma and abuse had brought me into incredible despair. I no longer wanted to live. I did not like my life. I felt worthless, shame, guilt, and so much pain. At the same time, my schooling suffered, and I went from academic probation to academic suspension. I had to withdraw from school, and I was not allowed to re-enroll for two semesters.

Meanwhile, I was trying to survive a severely abusive relationship. And at the same time, I had to confront my drinking. I started to lose all hope.

One night, I had a very vivid dream. I had a dream of being in *C'iggiz*. I was in my grandmother Julie's home. She was exactly as I remembered her. She had a small flower-designed dress, and her bangs were pinned back with black bobby pins. She had dark rectangular glasses, and she was wearing knitted slippers with pom-poms. I sat on her couch, and she was walking back and forth in the living room. She was speaking to me in Wet'suwet'en. At that time in my life, I could not understand the language. As she spoke, I buried my face in my hands, and I wept. I was nodding my head, and as she continued to speak Wet'suwet'en, I cried and said: "Yes. I know … I know … "

It was shortly after that when I decided to stop drinking. I did not want to die, so I went to detox and then to treatment. I had such a hard time trying to change my lifestyle. The second and last time I went to detox, I stayed for a few days. I was so sick! One of the detox staff comforted me, and she said: "I know it feels like you are going to die, but you aren't! You are going to be okay." A few days later, I had recovered from being so sick. One of my brothers picked me up and asked if I wanted to go to a storytelling event at the University of British Columbia First Nations House of Learning. I no longer had a place to live, I no longer had a relationship, I didn't have anywhere to go, and I did not know what I was going to do. So, I agreed. My life was in shambles. I tried to sit through the storytelling in the best way I could. The storyteller was Chief Dan George's son, Chief Leonard George of the *Tsleil-Waututh* Nation. After the session, I asked if I could speak to him. We went to the corner of the longhouse, and I shared with him in a very short period of time all that I had been through. I cried and told him that I felt like I lost my spirit. I said that there was a song that he sings that brings me peace: the "Prayer Song." I asked if he could sing it. He took a deep breath and sang so loud and clear that it echoed through the longhouse. As he sang, tears flowed down my face. After he sang, he looked up at me and said: "You didn't lose your spirit. If you lost your spirit, there wouldn't be tears." That was the start of my new journey. That was in April 1995. It was around this time in my life that I also finally found the courage to finally leave that relationship, never to return. Once again, it was those who chose to acknowledge me, support me, and encourage me that saved my life. My friend and mentor Barb walked with me through my pain and my turmoil and helped me see that there was a better way. I needed to change my life and embrace ways that were life-giving.

Images & Figures

FIGURE 1   1931—Sam George and Felix George at
the opening of Hagwilget Bridge (Tse Kya).

Photo from the George family

FIGURE 2   Julie and Paddy Isaac at C'iggiz.

Photo from George family photo collection.

FIGURE 3   Gisdaywa and Tsaybesa.

Photo from the George family photo collection.

FIGURE 4   Totem poles at Toody-Ni.

Photo from the George family photo collection.

FIGURE 5   Gallahgun with Beh (smoked salmon).

Photo from the George family photo collection.

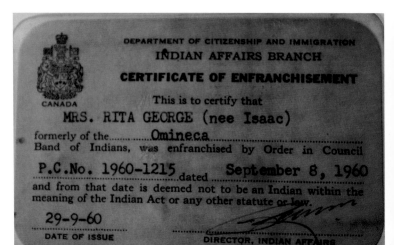

FIGURE 6   Rita George—Certificate of Enfranchisement.

Photo from the author.

FIGURE 7   Cover of Eulogy for Andrew George Sr.

Photo from the author.

FIGURE 8   Beh strips (smoked salmon).

Photo from the author.

FIGURE 9   Walk for Reconciliation 2013 Grand
Chief Stewart Phillip and Corinne.
Photo from Union of BC Indian Chiefs, Facebook,
https://www.facebook.com/**UBCIC**/photos.

FIGURE 10 Aikido training.

Photo from the author.

FIGURE 11 Paris Sensei and Corinne.

Photo from the author.

FIGURE 12 Keyikh Winiits (Nadina Mountain),
Gidimt'en Yintah.

Photo from the author.

FIGURE 13 Corinne snowshoeing on Gidimt'en Territory.

Photo from the author.

FIGURE 14 Seasonal rounds.

Photo from the author.

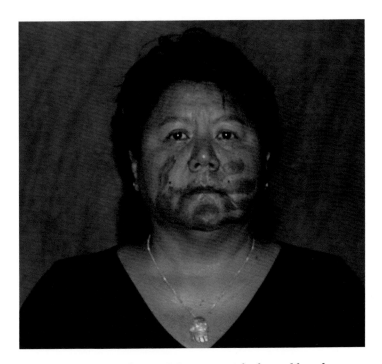

FIGURE 15 A photo of Corinne with the red hand symbolic of "Missing and Murdered Indigenous Women."

Photo from the author.

4

Healing

—

I knew it was critical for my physical, mental, emotional, and spiritual survival to reconnect with my ancestral ways. I started to make drums and I began to sing as often as I was able. I was never the best singer, but singing gave me life, and so I continue to sing.

Since 1995, I have taken many steps towards healing and reconnecting with the trails of my ancestors. At the heart of my healing was my reconnection to my strong foundation as a Wet'suwet'en woman. My ancestors needed to be central to my healing, and it was my reconnection to my ancestors and *Niwh Yintah* that was critical.

While on the initial path of healing, I took on a position working with youth, as even in the most challenging and difficult times of my life, working with youth still gave me life and hope. It made sense for me to continue on that path, so while maintaining my integrity and while continuing to be truthful about the challenges I confronted, I secured employment working with young people. It was an incredible opportunity as I was able to put into motion some concepts that I had already made sense of within myself, including keys ways of healing: to amplify a sense of belonging, sense of connection, and self-identity.

From the years of 1995 to 2000, I worked with youth alongside my own journey of healing. The work with the youth entailed drumming and singing, bringing them out on the land, and encouraging culture and identity in various ways. I needed to encourage some of the youth to use their voices to drum and sing. Initially, some of the youth were so shy (this I understood!) and did not feel comfortable singing in front of others. I accessed resources from other organizations and asked my sister-in-law Carla to share her songs. By the end of one year, the youth stood strong, confident, and powerful, and they sang in front of the leaders of the organization for which I was working at the time. It was absolutely beautiful and powerful!

As I worked with the youth, I was also on my own healing journey, striving to regain connection to my ancestors. I knew it was critical for my physical, mental, emotional, and spiritual survival to reconnect with my ancestral ways. This was part of this journey; I continued to heal in my own ways. I continued to pick up a drum and started to make drums, and I began to sing as often as I was able. I was never the best singer, but singing gave me life, and so I continue to sing.

In 1998, my father passed away. It was one of the most life-changing and painful days of my life. My mother phoned me while I was at work in Vancouver and told me that dad had just died. In immediate denial, I asked: "Are you sure?" As my mother wept, she explained what had happened and asked me to call my other siblings. This was one of the hardest things I had to do: to tell my siblings that our father had just died.

On the night of my father's passing, one of my brothers and I returned back home, flying from Vancouver to Smithers. I wept silently through the entire flight home. When we got back to *C'iggiz*, my mom and dad's home was surrounded by vehicles as the Wet'suwet'en Hereditary Chiefs and various members of the community gathered to be with mom and our family. When we walked into the house, Wet'suwet'en Hereditary Chiefs greeted us and comforted us. Our home was full. As broken-hearted as I was, I was so deeply touched by the expression of love and unity of the Chiefs as they displayed incredible respect for my beautiful matriarch and honour for my father. The gathering of the Chiefs upon the passing of someone among the Wet'suwet'en, particularly that of a highly respected elder and Hereditary Chief, has always been and still is very much part of our culture. Without going into too much detail about our *Balhats* system here, I will note that this is one of the ways our system takes care of each other. Our ancestors taught us to uphold and support each other, particularly when a loved one has passed over with the ancestors. These are memories that I deeply cherish. Upon entering our home, the Hereditary Chiefs and other clan members upheld us and walked with us through our journey of grief and mourning. When I first saw his eulogy, shown in figure 7 on page 62, my breath was taken as he was so regal and honourable.

My experience upon arriving back home after dad died was another reaffirmation as to the importance of my identity as a Wet'suwet'en woman and adherence to my culture and values. I was reminded of how our ancestors deeply loved and cared for each other. My father's influence among the Wet'suwet'en was far-reaching and strong. This was shown by the number of people who came when he passed away. My father's journey as a Hereditary Chief, hunter, trapper, knowledge holder, and WWII veteran became a lasting legacy. He continues to influence me each day.

While I engaged in our seasonal rounds all my life, regardless of what was happening, I made a stronger effort to engage more fully after 1995. Seasonal rounds have always been a great part of the Wet'suwet'en traditions and the connection to our territories. Seasonal rounds included but were not limited to harvesting and processing salmon, moose, and berries; collecting medicines; snaring rabbits; and trapping/hunting for various animals. Figure 8 on page 63 shows the results of our labour: Beh strips that would last us the year and to this day remain a delicacy. When residing in the city, my mom and dad always provided us with staples to assist us, and whenever possible, we would return home to help with seasonal rounds.

As I grew older, my connection to our seasonal rounds traditions intensified, as did my connection to *Niwh Yintah*. I will note that *Niwh Yintah* was always foundational and central for me, but as I got older, the oral histories and oral tradition became clearer for me as I started to draw the connections on the territories.

With the passing of my father and a reaffirmation of Wet'suwet'en culture and history, I started to focus on other aspects of my well-being. I felt a strong need to reconnect with spirituality and faith, as well as my physical

well-being. It made perfect sense for me to
reconnect spiritually with our ancestors and our
culture. This meant time on *Niwh Yintah* and
also at the *Balhats* hall. Furthermore, my ancestors were also very connected with the spiritual
and faith-based aspects of the Roman Catholic
Church. In essence, they connected with *Uttigai*
(the Creator), centred on our ancestral spirituality. Thus, I made a great effort to return home
whenever possible to spend more time on the
land again, as well as in the *Balhats* hall. I also
returned to church. I struggled with my return
to church, having become familiar with some
of the colonial aspects of our relationship with
the Church, but I was also aware of how some
of our ancestors were so strongly connected to
Uttigai through the Church. In particular, the
singing of Carrier Hymns has always been such
a powerful memory for me, a memory of faith,
spirit, humility, strength, and beauty. I clung
to this, and I was able to grieve my father and
stay strong. In the meantime, I focused on my
physical health, as well as other aspects of my
well-being.

As I walked, breathed, prayed, drummed, sang,
and continued to learn, I started to regain my
physical, emotional, mental, and spiritual health.
I have so many people to thank for my journey

of reconnection to drumming and singing, especially my sister-in-law Carla. I maintained a healthy lifestyle, and although involved in some relationships, in general, I remained single. In 1999, I formed a friendship with a man who eventually became my husband. We met in Vancouver, and shortly after we met and spent a great deal of time together in friendship, he left Vancouver. We wrote letters and realized that our friendship had blossomed, and we eventually married. John had been a Roman Catholic priest for many years, and he and I walked together in the spirit of faith. As with all relationships, ours was not without challenges. But our marriage was based on friendship, spirit, love, respect, honesty, truth, and honour. He continues to love, honour, respect, and uphold me as though I am in the palm of his hand. I am blessed.

Shortly after we married, we moved to Lethbridge, Alberta. Little did I realize how the nature of this new chapter in my life would shift my direction so dramatically. Our start in Lethbridge was very challenging as neither of us had employment, and we had very little resources for a fresh beginning. Despite this, we managed to secure a rental unit, and John went right to work. We did not have anything other than our clothing, so we had to borrow a foam mattress from our new property owner until we were able to afford a bed. Little by little, we were able to furnish and make Lethbridge our new home for the start of our marriage.

It was at this time in my life that I decided it was time to go back to school to finish what I had started. While John was at work, I went to the University of Lethbridge and made an appointment with an academic advisor. I spoke with the advisor about my previous experiences in post-secondary institutions, which resulted in academic suspension. I provided him with a copy of my unofficial transcripts, and he exclaimed that I had a great number of transferrable credits and that I could potentially have about two years of credits. I said, "Yes, but I am sure I am too late to start in January." He said, "No, actually, you have enough time to get together your official transcripts and apply!" That was it! I started the ball rolling and did everything I could to get back into school. I was determined, although I was unsure as to how I would pay for it all, so I immediately applied for student loans. I secured student loans and then also supplemented my income with Band sponsorship. I enrolled to continue with a Bachelor of Arts with a desire to earn credits and work towards a

Bachelor of Education. My intent was to become a high school history teacher.

Going back to school as a mature student with experience made a great deal of difference for me. Kudos to those with the ability to complete a degree right from high school to post-secondary! I fully embraced my renewed opportunity, and with every history course I enrolled in, I ensured to offer an Aboriginal perspective. I started to understand the history, dynamics, and circumstances that influenced the relationship between global populations and Aboriginal people in Canada. I realized the importance of learning other histories in order to understand relationships more fully. As I wrote papers and researched, I discovered a new passion. In one of my courses, "History of Western Canada," I read a book on the syllabus called *Aboriginal People and Colonizers of Western Canada* by Sarah Carter. One line in the book was so eloquently stated that I was taken aback: "European explorers didn't really 'explore' at all. Rather, they were taken on guided tours, often along well-traveled routes. In the history of North America, Aboriginal women, as well as men, played remarkable roles as guides and interpreters."[10] To challenge the narrative of the role of "explorers" and to acknowledge the roles of Aboriginal women was not only insightful but also bold in the face of some conservative viewpoints of history. I was intrigued.

My coursework in the discipline of history was very diverse, ranging from European history to the history of Latin America to Canadian History. The entire time, I chose to focus on the Aboriginal perspective and chose essay topics to highlight those histories. For example, when engaging in a survey course in American history, I wrote about the Cherokee Trail of Tears and presented my paper to the class. I found the history of the right wing in Canada a very significant and important course to help me understand some of the strained and most challenging relations between Aboriginal people and non-Aboriginal people. I started to gain a tremendous understanding of historical tensions in Canada.

As I continued my schooling, I spent more time researching, particularly in the archives. My passion for learning more about historical relationships and circumstances deepened. I remembered Sarah Carter's book and how her perspective intrigued me. I started to consider the possibility of a Master of Arts (MA) degree. One day, I connected with Sarah Carter while on an afternoon visit to the University of

Calgary. I told her about my desire to pursue an MA. She asked me to stay in touch, which I did. From that moment on, I continued to do the best I could, working in the library until the library closed, knowing that I needed to have a higher grade point average to get into graduate school. I worked very hard to achieve my next academic goal.

It was during this time that I was reminded of a famous quote from Chief Dan George: "Oh God! Like the thunderbird of old I shall rise again out of the sea; I shall grab the instruments of the white man's success—his education, his skills, and with these new tools I shall build my race into the proudest segment of your society." This quote spoke to me and inspired me to continue on my academic journey.

In the meantime, I also needed to remain mindful of my physical and spiritual well-being. I connected with Aboriginal elders from the region. One day in December 2002, I sought out a martial art with which to engage as I had always wanted to participate in one. I came upon a brochure for "Aikido," which is known as the "Way of Harmony." My husband and I participated in an introductory session and decided to continue training. Aikido training was very complex, and I had a difficult time, but I was determined to continue. One day after practice, I told my husband, "I am not cut out for Aikido. I don't think I want to continue." He said, "Okay. How about try one more practice tonight and if you still feel the same way, then we will stop." I agreed and ended up having a great training session. So, I carried on. Many aspects of Aikido philosophy aligned with universal Indigenous philosophy. This is part of the reason why I was so attracted to Aikido. I will be forever grateful for this introduction to Aikido.

Excelling in my schoolwork, training in Aikido, a connection to culture and spirituality, and my husband's support brought me through to the completion of my Bachelor of Arts Degree. When I graduated from my BA program, I was very emotional as I never thought I would see the day that I would graduate from university. When I had moved towards the completion of my BA, I connected with Sarah Carter and applied to grad school at the University of Calgary. I was accepted and started to consider my Master of Arts degree topic.

When John and I moved to Calgary so I could start my MA at the University of Calgary, I was excited and somewhat afraid. I never, in my wildest dreams, thought I would pursue a Master of Arts degree. While completing my first-year requirements, I narrowed down my initial topic and decided to focus on "Grassroots Activism of Aboriginal Women in Calgary and Edmonton, 1951–1985." I looked at the intersections of the Indian Act, Aboriginal women, and oral histories. I wanted to highlight and celebrate the achievements of Aboriginal women and Aboriginal people, more generally.

My MA journey in history was so insightful, intriguing, and intense. I sought to gather oral histories of Aboriginal women in Calgary and Edmonton who were involved in grassroots activism. It did not take long for me to locate those eager to share their stories. It was an incredible honour to enjoy tea and sit with these Aboriginal women, these elders who endured so many challenges. They were all so strong and beautiful. I wrote their stories with the highest respect, honour, and integrity. These women faced too much turmoil, pain, and trauma and yet retained a strong connection to their cultures and identities while engaging in political, social, and economic activism.

As I worked towards completion of my MA, I had to dig deep. It was such a great challenge. One of the major challenges was a second language requirement and I chose French as it was the language I knew most about at that time

other than English. One of the requirements
for the completion of the MA was to translate
a historical text from French to English—in a
scholarly style, and loose translations would not
be acceptable. I had to work very hard to ensure
success for my language requirement. This was
only one of the many challenges. I was almost
ready to give up because it was so incredibly
hard. I phoned my mother one night and I wept;
I said: "I am not sure if I can do this! I am ready
to give up. This is so hard!!" Mom was quiet for a
while. She then started to tell me a story about
my grandpa *Gisdaywa* (Thomas George). When
the economy started to shift, he took on a job
working for the Grand Trunk Railway. His duties
included using a pack horse through the canyons.
The canyon trails were narrow and windy, and
the walls were steep; one misstep and he and the
horse would perish into the canyon. He brought
this experience back to his family and used it as
an analogy for life: *N'tsay tsi-yilth, awht'siy yilth.*
My mom translated this to me: "Where we are
going, we must keep going (we must not give
up!!)." This was all I needed to hear. I completed
my Master of Arts degree in History a few
months later. By this time, I had already sent
out applications to continue my schooling with
a PhD in History. My intent was to move back

to British Columbia and complete a PhD focused on BC history.

I felt so happy and confident as we moved back to BC as I had accepted a scholarship to Simon Fraser University to start my PhD. Residing in the Lower Mainland was (and still is) so awfully expensive, so I sought assistance in every way possible. Upon arrival back to Vancouver and the Lower Mainland, I could not stop thinking about my previous years spent there. In particular, I knew that I needed to visit Chief Leonard George of the *Tsleil-Waututh* Nation to share my journey with him. I visited him at his home, and I reminded him of the time he sang the Prayer Song to me at the University of British Columbia's (UBC) First Nations House of Learning and that, at that time, my life was in turmoil. I reminded him that he told me that I did not lose my spirit, that if I lost my spirit, there wouldn't be tears. I gave him some tobacco, and I requested permission to use the Prayer Song. He said: "Well, let me hear it!" So, I drew a deep breath and sang at the top of my lungs. He was pleased, and he said: "That is not quite the way we sing it, but your heart is in a good place," and he gave me permission to sing the Prayer Song as I was able to sing it. I often sing the

Prayer Song when I need to and, in particular, when I share this part of my life experience.

My intent for my PhD was to focus on the Wet'suwet'en. I wanted to gather oral histories about an aspect of the Indian Act (springing from my MA thesis), primarily the McKenna-McBride Commission, as it related to the Wet'suwet'en hereditary system. These issues were outlined in the landmark *Delgamuukw/Gisdaywa* court case. I specifically wanted to interview a number of Wet'suwet'en elders, all of whom have since passed away, with the exception of my mother. I completed my PhD coursework and aced the courses. I was thrilled, not only because I completed the coursework and did extremely well, but also because I learned so much—again! For example, one of the courses I took focused on the Arctic peoples, and I captured a glimpse of the history of the North. I realize it was only a heartbeat in history, but again, I was so intrigued.

I was also so happy to accept a position as a teaching assistant in a second-year Canadian history course, as well as an online course, "The British Empire and Commonwealth." I felt confident in my knowledge and continued to learn and embrace all that I was able to do. I was on top of the world. This feeling of achievement

carried through with me as I studied for my
comprehensive exams. I studied so hard for my
exams as I put in easily fifteen-hour days and
read about 150 books. The day came when I was
to start writing my comprehensive exams. I
felt ready, but I was also aware that the nature
of the exams was critical, and if I did not pass,
that would be the end of my academic journey. I
wrote the exams one by one, which were centred
on three streams: oral history, the social/
cultural history of Canada, and a comparative
study of the American/Canadian legal history of
Aboriginal people. I eagerly awaited the outcome
of my comprehensive exams. Finally, I received
an e-mail asking me to contact my supervisor. I
called her and the short call comprised of: "Hi
Corinne! I am sorry, but you did not pass your
comprehensive exams. You passed one but
not the other two … sorry!" Our conversation
felt harried and she did not seem interested in
giving me any more time than was necessary.
My heart shattered. At that moment, my dream
of completing a PhD in history was completely
gone. When I asked her why, her response was
subjective and consisted of two words. In hind-
sight, her level of support was minimal at best,
my Wet'suwet'en worldview was not honoured,
and the subjective results of my comprehensive

exams were based on Western understandings. Furthermore, when I attempted to work with my PhD supervisor, I felt insignificant and that I was a bother. My reaction to these moments was to continue to forge ahead despite the low level of support from my then PhD supervisor. Ultimately, my efforts to forge ahead were futile.

After receiving the news that I could no longer continue with a PhD, I cried for days. I was in shock as I had worked so hard for seven years to get to that point. I am still not over this heartbreak, and although I have been asked by other institutions/entities to continue with a PhD, I am unable to. I am grateful that the Truth and Reconciliation Commission's calls to action have put into place safeguards for those like me who wish to uphold ancestral and traditional knowledge.

While I understand that not everyone can complete a PhD and that its completion requires a certain level of Western intellect coupled with a high degree of institutional and academic prowess, I knew that I had the ability to fulfil the requirements. From the time I went back to school to that moment, my average grade was "A-minus." Moreover, my ability to navigate both Western and Traditional education provided a very strong backdrop for my proposed topic. It is very unfortunate—sad—traumatic—that systemic and institutional barriers prevented me from continuing my PhD journey.

I had to try to pick up the pieces of my heart and carry on. First and foremost, I needed to find employment as my husband had been working so hard while I attended school. I looked for quite some time until I found a place of employment that focused on my expertise: archival research and Aboriginal history. I was thrilled when I received a call back from the Union of BC Indian Chiefs (UBCIC) for a position as a researcher. Again, I was exposed to incredible learning as I delved into pockets of the history of Aboriginal people in BC. Having had exposure to research during my BA and MA, I was introduced to a new level of research. In addition to our roles and responsibilities as researchers, we supported the mandate and vision of UBCIC. We participated in the Missing and Murdered Indigenous Women's Marches on February 14 on the Downtown Eastside of Vancouver every year, we marched in opposition to Enbridge, we fully participated in Idle No More events, and we also took part in the 2013 Walk for Truth and Reconciliation where over 70,000 people marched on the streets of Vancouver (see figure 9 on page 64). At this event, Dr. Martin Luther King Jr.'s daughter spoke. She stated: "Social change cannot come overnight, yet it causes one to work as if it was a possibility the next morning. I encourage you as you continue to move forward. This is going to be a long journey, but every journey begins with a step. Believe it or not, you have made a big step towards progress here in Canada."[11]

I spent a great deal of time with Grand Chief Stewart Phillip as I shared my family history and personal experiences with him. He always acknowledged me and so graciously offered me time in his very busy schedule. He had become a mentor who always upheld Aboriginal women. I am very grateful for his ongoing influence in my life. I am very grateful that to him, I am neither invisible nor marginal and that our friendship is based on an incredible level of mutual respect.

I continued to also focus on my physical well-being during this time. One of my addictions was tackling the Grouse Grind, which is a 2.9 km walk straight up the face of Grouse Mountain in Vancouver. I signed up for the "Grind for Kids" which was a fundraiser for BC Children's Hospital. I participated in the "Grind for Kids" for two years; my record of most "Grouse Grinds" in one day is three. That was my limit. Often, I would wake up at 5:30 a.m. and make my way to

Grouse Mountain and climb the Grouse Grind before work. I also started to cycle commute and very much enjoyed it.

In addition to my other physical activities, I continued training in Aikido. With my mother aging, I knew that someday I would move back to Northern BC, so I decided that I would start testing to rank so that I would be able to "bring Aikido home with me." My Sensei, who at the time had been practicing Aikido for over twenty-five years, became one of my mentors. As with all Senseis, he was demanding and guided his students to train to the highest of their abilities. Figure 10 on page 65 highlights a moment of Aikido training, showing me executing "kokye nage," one of the various forms used to transfer an attacker's energy. Paris Sensei took me under his wing and guided me through my successful test for Nidan in Aikido, a second-degree Black Belt. The test for Nidan was gruelling and was physically, mentally, emotionally, and spiritu-ally a tremendous challenge. Upon successful completion, I was very emotional as the test and the training for the Nidan were among the most challenging tests of my life. I will be forever grateful to my Sensei, who believed in me and guided me forward. I continue to embrace

Aikido and the philosophy of Aikido aligns with my values and principles.

Figure 11 on page 66 is a photo of Paris Sensei and me. I will be forever grateful to Paris Sensei for believing in me and seeing me and my abilities. Osawa Sensei, from Japan, tested me for my Nidan and was very demanding. Successful completion of my Nidan test has been one of the most important experiences in my life.

O'Sensei, Aikido's founder, based this way on harmony and peace. Aikido means "The Way of Harmony." Aikido aligns with so many values that I strive to embrace, including the values of my ancestors. O'Sensei said:

Create each day anew by clothing yourself with heaven and earth, bathing yourself with wisdom and love, and placing yourself in the heart of Mother Nature. Your body and mind will be gladdened, depression and heartache will dissipate, and you will be filled with gratitude.[12]

I left UBCIC and Vancouver in 2015 and moved back home to *C'iggiz* to be with my mother. It was a very challenging move for my husband and me, but we were also both very aware that someone needed to be with my mother as she was getting older and residing alone was getting more and more difficult for her. My mother spent several years on her own in *C'iggiz* after my father passed away, but we knew it was time for someone to be at her side. So, we decided to leave Vancouver and head north.

5

Reconnecting with the Trails of My Ancestors

—

> *Among the many lessons of our ancestors that my mother and father passed on to us was that we always needed to be respectful of other clan territories... I strive to walk softly and respectfully not only on our own clan territory but especially when I visit other territories.*

Moving back home to *C'iggiz* was the best decision I ever made in my life. Although I had resided on Wet'suwet'en territory for a few months here and there as an adult, for much of twenty-five years since leaving high school, I resided in Metro Vancouver. I had always retained a strong connection with my ancestors no matter what; however, upon returning home, my connection has grown in so many ways and on so many levels. Walking with my mother, my matriarch, has deepened and broadened my knowledge of who we are as Wet'suwet'en and being at my matriarch's side at this time in my life is a tremendous honour. Connection to my culture and my identity softened the impacts of colonization and has given me strength, courage, hope, and guidance.

Upon moving back home, I was immediately physically reconnected to my culture as I spent a great deal of time in various *Balhats* and time on *Niwh Yintah*. Those moments of great turmoil, pain, and challenge floated away when I reached back in my memory, heart, and soul to *Keyikh Winiits* (Nadina Mountain). My grandpa *Gisdaywa, Keyikh Winiits, Gidimt'en Yintah* all became physically within reach, and I started to spend as much possible time as I could on the territories. Here is only a glimpse of the landmark territories that have always been part of my heart and soul and all that I have visited in my heart throughout the greatest challenges of my life. I walked, snowshoed, kayaked, and hiked the *Yintah*.

My memory and vision of this mountain brought me through so much. It has been such a blessing to be able to physically visit Nadina Mountain and my ancestors whenever possible. Every time I visit this mountain, and especially when I climb this mountain, I can feel the presence of my ancestors so strongly. I took this photo (figure 12 on page 67) on a beautiful, calm, and peaceful morning at about 6 a.m. on Bi winii (Owen Lake), Gidimt'en territory, where my paternal ancestors thrived and where our family has spent so much time. My mother shared oral history with me about how my grandfather Gisdaywa spoke of the feeling that we, as Wet'suwet'en, have when we spend time on our territories. I will forever hold her oral history in my heart.

The little mountain on which I am standing in figure 13 on page 68 has deep, deep historical and ancestral significance for me and my maternal ancestors. My mother shared a great deal of oral history with me as regards this exact location on *Niwh Yintah*. My husband John and I often snowshoe to this spot and enjoy some tea. As always, quiet time, reflection, and a visit with my ancestors calm my spirit and refresh my soul.

The imprints of our childhood and youth on *Niwh Yintah* were intensely critical for us as we grew into adulthood and navigated through life. No matter what, we always returned to the territories for our seasonal rounds. Our seasonal rounds, after all, were how we survived as a family. When residing away from Wet'suwet'en territory, I always returned for summer seasonal rounds. But, when I moved back home, I was able to fully engage. For example, catching trout in the spring was critical for our survival (figure 14 on page 69). We needed to eat, and therefore, we had to fish for trout every year. Spring trout was one of the main staples among the Wet'suwet'en and this has always been one of our family food staples.

Over the last several years, I have been snaring rabbits for my mother as fried rabbit and rabbit stew are among her favourite traditional delicacies. One day, when I returned from checking the snares, she was looking out the kitchen window and was very emotional. She told me: "When I was a little girl, I used to follow behind my mother as she set snares and checked her snares. Little did I know that years later, her granddaughter would be doing the same thing." Walking on the trails of my ancestors gives me life, gives me strength, and gives me guidance. The influence of my ancestors remains strong within me.

Among the many lessons of our ancestors that my mother and father passed on to us was that we always needed to be respectful of other clan territories. While we had been given permission to access some territories that were outside our clans, we always made sure that we respected territorial boundaries. It was a very important lesson from our ancestors. I strive to walk softly and respectfully not only on our own clan territory but especially when I visit other territories. From a young age, mom and dad made sure we were aware of the various territorial boundaries and the oral histories connected to them. I choose not to share many of these stories in written form because there are so many oral histories that are important to keep within the oral tradition. Once something is written down, it changes the integrity and nature of the oral tradition, and then its sacredness is compromised. I will certainly respect this nature and maintain sacred oral histories in that realm.

Although the nature of the *Balhats* had been part of our beings since the day we were born, moving back home gave me the opportunity to once again become fully immersed. I started to support my mother in every way possible to prepare for upcoming *Balhats;* preparing salmon and moose, harvesting various types of berries, and assisting with gift purchases for our Father Clan. My mother started to teach more fully. There is so much to learn, and I was once again reminded as to why it takes a lifetime to learn and understand our culture. I was very fortunate that mom and dad walked with us on *Niwh Yintah* when we were babies and that we learned so much from our childhood and retained all those teachings. The *Balhats* is central for the Wet'suwet'en; it is our law, our territories, our kinship, and our economy. I have been honoured and blessed to learn from our matriarchs, particularly from my mother, because she was groomed for years by many of our highly respected Chiefs. Because of my involvement in the *Balhats* and standing with my mother, my mother had prepared me for a feast name that I currently hold. I strive to do my best to ensure that I hold this name as my ancestors held theirs … with truth, honour, respect, and dignity.

Upon moving back to *C'iggiz,* I started work at the College of New Caledonia (CNC) in Burns Lake. Among my roles: teaching Wet'suwet'en culture and history to a number of youth enrolled in a program. I absolutely loved every moment because I very much enjoy teaching, but having the opportunity to teach the basics of Wet'suwet'en culture and history was very special. My roles at CNC-Burns Lake Campus varied and shifted through time. Regardless of my roles, my vision and focus remained the same: to highlight the voices of Aboriginal people, to do whatever I can to enhance relationships between Aboriginal and non-Aboriginal members of the community, and to indigenize wherever possible. I started a leadership role within the College as the Regional Principal of the Burns Lake Campus, which did not occur without a great deal of discernment. When the opportunity arose, I had wondered if I would be able to engage in the leadership opportunity. I walked on the territories, considering whether I would be able to do the job. I decided to apply, thinking that it would be a great opportunity to indigenize and foster relationships between Aboriginal and non-Aboriginal community members, thereby having a part in facilitating Truth and Reconciliation calls to action at the institutional level. Much like many of my life ventures, my time at the College can be characterized as success sprinkled with victories but also with various challenges. I have been very grateful for this experience, and because of this experience, I have been able to continue to understand the dynamics between Aboriginal and non-Aboriginal people. There is so much to learn.

Shortly after moving back to *C'iggiz*, my mother was diagnosed with cancer. Mom underwent chemotherapy and radiation and also had to undergo two surgeries. This was extremely hard on her, and there were many moments when John and I were not sure if she would make it. I can't even begin to say how many times I brought mom into Emergency during this time because she was dehydrated and so very ill. One of these times, mom was very, very sick, and the Emergency department was overloaded at the Prince George hospital.

It was so overloaded, but they also knew that my mother was in very rough shape, so they brought her in. Her bed was wheeled right next to the nurse's station because all the spaces in the Emergency room were filled. I sat at the foot of her bed, and I was weeping because mom was so sick. Out of all the busyness and chaos of the Emergency room, I looked across the hall, and one elderly non-Aboriginal woman was watching me. Even though she was obviously busy with her own family, she got up and walked over to me and asked me what was happening. I told her and explained that mom was undergoing chemotherapy and radiation and that she was very, very sick. This beautiful person embraced me and told me to take good care of myself, and wished us the best. There are some very kind-hearted people in this world. My mother had a very challenging few years with her cancer journey. As of 2023, her reports indicate that she remains cancer free. It is truly an honour to continue to learn from my matriarch and to walk at her side.

In the last few years, I have started learning to speak Wet'suwet'en. Since I was young, my ability to speak or understand Wet'suwet'en was very limited because as a result of her experiences, my mother chose not to teach her children how to speak Wet'suwet'en. I have worked with my mother to learn our language. I am so grateful to say that I can now speak more Wet'suwet'en than I ever have, and when in the Feast Hall, I am able to generally grasp an understanding of all that is being conducted. I have so much to learn but I feel so blessed to learn the language from my matriarch.

Since moving back to Wet'suwet'en territory, I continued to spend more and more time on *Niwh Yintah* and in the *Balhats*. I have worked alongside my matriarchs and continue to work with my beautiful mom and strive to learn all that I am able to; there is so much to learn! A few years ago, my matriarchs wanted me to receive a Wet'suwet'en name. I was reluctant. However, I eventually remembered that it is important to be in a position of service for the people, for the community, and for the good of who we are as Wet'suwet'en. I needed to step up to help my mother and my clan and do all that we are able for our Nation. So, I received a name in 2021: *Sus Binii Hilthtus*. This means: "A Bear with a Strong Mind." I stood with my matriarchs upon receipt of my name. I shed tears of joy because of all that I had gone through and because I knew in my heart and soul that my ancestors guided me all along the way. I wept because I understood that it takes a lifetime of learning to receive such an honour. From the moment I walked on *Niwh Yintah,* I started to learn, and I continued to learn throughout my whole life to that point. I understand why it takes a lifetime to earn a Wet'suwet'en name. That said, there is so much more to learn.

6

Conclusion: Truth...and then Reconciliation

—

> *Of course, I have made many mistakes throughout my life. Having gone through incredible trauma does not give reason to mistreat or harm others. This is not only something I need to remember, but this is a message that is critically important for all.*

This is my truth. I was born in 1971 in Wet'suwet'en territory, in Smithers, BC, and was raised at *Toody-Ni* just outside of Telkwa. I am Wet'suwet'en and Gitksan from the *Gidimt'en* clan, and I come from a long line of Hereditary Chiefs and elected leaders. I am the daughter of two very traditional parents, one of whom was also a residential school survivor and one who was a veteran of WWII. As a result of colonization, I encountered incredible levels of trauma, and my strength, courage, and dignity arose from the Spirit of my ancestors. Despite the historical impacts of colonization and trauma, my connection to my ancestral ways and my identity have been critical. This is how I survived and how I strive to thrive.

The truth is that I have been blessed with a good life and have had the good fortune to have connected with some amazing people with very kind hearts who have loved me and accepted me for who I am, first as a Wet'suwet'en girl and later a Wet'suwet'en woman. In order to achieve reconciliation, it is important to acknowledge the truth, as outlined in the Truth and Reconciliation Commission. Since I was a little girl, some of the most painful truths can be categorized in the following themes: historical and personal trauma connected to colonialism, racism and my experiences as a Wet'suwet'en woman, institutional and systemic racism, and lateral violence and the painful reality of "being silenced."

Historical trauma connected to colonialism has had an extreme impact on my life from the time I was a little girl, including childhood sexual abuse and the historical impacts of being a daughter of a residential school survivor. The experiences of sexual abuse from an early age affected me and my life. Holding on to a secret of sexual abuse for over forty years resulted in my inability to trust, lack of social skills, and inability to speak of the pain associated with the abuse. It has affected my ability to form or maintain healthy relationships. I felt ashamed, and as a result, my self-esteem and self-confidence suffered. I had always been afraid to share this truth because I did not want to be stigmatized. I did not want others to view me as if there was something wrong with me. As I am able to share more with others about my pain and my experiences, I have gathered self-awareness and every time I speak about my trauma, I heal a little bit more. It is a very long road of healing but I am taking this one step at a time.

As a Wet'suwet'en female born and raised on what is now known as the "Highway of Tears," it was not uncommon to receive inferior treatment. There were times when I was overtly targeted: "I hate Indians," or as some drove down the main street yelling "Fucking Squaw!!" out the window of their vehicle. It was also very common for people to outwardly refuse to acknowledge my existence as a human being. My self-esteem and confidence were affected as a result of this type of disrespect. My integrity, dignity, and strength in my identity as a Wet'suwet'en girl/woman were critical, and my connection to my ancestors and my culture has always been my stronghold.

Identity theft and theft of culture are two realities that are elements of historical trauma. So many of us have already gone through incredible trauma, but there are some who take it further and steal our identities. Those who do so are called "Pretendians." The actions of those stealing our Indigenous identities are so troublesome and retraumatizing because we have gone through so much, and there are now some who claim identity to take advantage of the steps towards reconciliation, without ever having had to endure the same trauma. I would hope that those who falsely claim Aboriginal identity realize that through identity theft, you are stealing our chances of thriving.

It is also important to note that at this time in our lives, there are also those who hijack cultures for their own agendas. This harsh reality is akin to colonialism, giving the hijacked culture a sense of being "re-colonized." So, when the hijacking of a culture occurs, a collective sense of trauma pervades a nation. In order for a nation to heal, we need to maintain a strong sense of unity and hold strong to our culture as a nation without outside influences.

Institutional and systemic racism presented itself in many forms throughout my life. From preschool through to high school, I was one of the few Aboriginal people in non-Aboriginal educational institutions. I did not know until years later that by the time I reached school age, that the residential school era had just passed (for the most part, although the last residential school closed around 1996). It now makes sense that, with some exceptions, I was treated and viewed so differently. Up until the 1970s, for the most part, Aboriginal people were segregated from mainstream education systems. This meant that Aboriginal and non-Aboriginal people had not yet mixed in the public school system. As a result of the segregated educational approach through the residential school system, there was a clash between Aboriginal and non-Aboriginal people. Racial tension was a prominent feature as I attended school from elementary through to post-secondary.

Among the various institutional and systemic realities was the feeling of being an outsider and the feeling of being alienated. Throughout my life, I was treated as invisible, not only in academic settings but in work settings as well; there were many who treated me as though I did not exist. That style of treatment—disrespect and marginalization—has been among the most painful experiences. This remains a reality for me, but I am learning to move forward despite this style of dynamic. But this type of treatment is torturous.

I do not deserve to be treated like I do not exist.

In essence, I need to navigate the two realities of the Aboriginal and non-Aboriginal and harmonize (Aikido taught me how to harmonize) as opposed to clash. Thus, retaining a connection to my identity as a Wet'suwet'en woman while striving to co-exist within non-Aboriginal

settings became an important aspect of the
journey. Much like my ancestors, who walked
well in both worlds, I also needed to navigate
both worlds. This was critically important for
my survival. I have proven that I can survive
and thrive in the Aboriginal world, but I often
stumble when I walk in the non-Aboriginal
world. This makes sense because I have a
different worldview, perspective, culture, history,
style of communication, and values. So, I need
to retain a strong sense of my identity and
my culture and occupy spaces that Aboriginal
people historically did not occupy. This can be
an incredible challenge, particularly when forced
to stand alone in the face of adversity, challenge,
and violence. When I graduated with my Master
of Arts degree, I figuratively held my degree in
one hand and held a hand drum in the other.

Unfortunately, one of the by-products of
colonialism is lateral violence. While so many
hope to move beyond lateral violence, we also
need to acknowledge the truth of lateral violence
and heal from it. I have been targeted so badly
by lateral violence. I have crossed paths with
many mean-spirited people. There have been
those who have mistreated me and refused to
acknowledge my existence as a human being.
Further, in my position of leadership, I have had

awful letters written about me and my family (many of which were from "anonymous" writers and were not signed). These types of dynamics are cruel and violent. In addition, there have been some who have shared stories of me and my family or my mother that were simply untrue and attempted to discredit and tear them apart. After all that I have been through in my life, I do not deserve this type of treatment.

One of the most painful realities that I have faced as a Wet'suwet'en woman is having been silenced on so many levels and in so many different ways throughout my life. It is unfortunate—critically unfortunate—that I have either been directly or indirectly silenced in connection with abuse, assault, impacts of colonialism (i.e., politics), lateral violence, or racism, including but not limited to systemic and institutional racism.

Being silenced is a very painful experience. I will outline some examples of the ways in which I have been silenced. In the past, when I was abused or assaulted, I was told not to tell anyone. This resulted in years of remaining silent, left to deal with my pain and shame in silence. Figure 15 on page 70 shows the red hand symbolism connected to being silenced which has been historically a direct link to the issue of Missing and Murdered Indigenous Women. As a Wet'suwet'en woman, I have been silenced in so many ways. This was torturous, and I have come to realize that it is critically important to speak about these occurrences to heal. I need to note here that I chose to make my story public, but not everyone needs to be *this* open about their past experiences. Sometimes, it might only be one or two people who you trust, or it might be a professional therapist who will remain unaffected. Either way, it is critically important to heal. I have taken these steps of healing, and I work with Dr. Martine, a trauma therapist, who very much understands and has studied trauma and is able to hear me and provide me with a much-needed understanding of how my experiences can affect me today. I am aware of the nature of how trauma from early childhood, as well as past ongoing trauma, can affect me today. Awareness is part of the healing journey.

Another instance of being silenced includes the notion of "professionalism" in Western institutions. When I was told that I was no longer able to continue with my PhD, I was in so much pain. But, because I was unable to share what really happened, due to fear of perceived judgement of who I am and my abilities, I chose to remain silent. This dynamic has been a common experience for me as I have faced so many who have mistreated me, disrespected me, and completely refused to acknowledge my existence as a human being. But, due to "professional constraints" I was limited in my ability to fully confront the circumstances in healthy ways. So, I am calling out the proverbial elephant in the living room and speaking my truth about the way I was treated when pursuing a PhD. Our knowledge, our history, our culture, and our worldviews are critical in forging ahead in our respective relationships. While things continue to change, I am hopeful that as we unveil these truths, we continue to seek reconciliation.

I have been silenced in political spheres. In an effort to share my perspective and my voice, I have been blocked from social media platforms. When there was a pipeline dispute on Gidimt'en territory, and I wanted to share my views as a Gidimt'en woman, I was blocked from sharing my viewpoints. I will never forget the day that, as a Gidimt'en woman alongside my matriarch, we sought to speak our truth on Gidimt'en Yintah, were swarmed by non-Gidimt'en/non-Wet'suwet'en, and we were told to "be quiet." My mother, a Gidimt'en woman and a respected Gidimt'en matriarch who has held a name in the *Balhats* since 1960, experienced repercussions and re-traumatization stemming from that moment and it was a hurtful reminder of so much we had to endure through our history. Further, awful letters were written about me, and members of my family and my place of employment were implicated. Being violently silenced has been an incredibly painful and traumatic experience.

These forms of lateral violence are not the answer. During one of my many conversations with Grand Chief Stewart Phillip, he stated, "We need to reconcile with each other first." Although I have certainly been caught up in unhealthy dynamics, I very much strive for healing, hope, and peace. I know that I fall short often, but when I stumble, I get back up and continue to do the best I can and continue to follow the trails of my ancestors.

At this time of Truth, it is important to remember that we need to sit with the truth for a while as we move towards Reconciliation. My story and my experiences are only one of an individual. I have come to realize that so many of us are still in pain, and we are still striving to heal. While so many are rushing towards Reconciliation, we have so much work to do with Truth. I share my story and my experiences not for pity, not for attention, but to convey that through my story, you might understand that there are so many who have similar stories, similar pain, and similar truths. I want to speak to those who have undergone similar trauma and tell you that you are not alone. I am hopeful that, through sharing my story and experiences, non-Indigenous people will gain insight and understanding about who we are as Aboriginal people and all that we endured. Further, I hope that, through sharing my experience, I shed light on understanding and truth but also hope on our collective journey towards Reconciliation.

In this journey of truth, while striving for reconciliation, it is more critical than ever to cling to the ways of my ancestors. I need to acknowledge my truth and speak my truth. I also need to remain accountable to myself and my ancestors while maintaining respect for others. Of course, I have made many mistakes through-out my life. Having gone through incredible trauma does not give reason to mistreat or harm others. This is not only something I need to remember, but this is a message that is critically important for all. Mistreating others because of colonial impacts or trauma is not the answer. Easier said than done. I am aware that when triggered, I fall short, but I am trying so hard to not be the person to mistreat or disrespect others. Sometimes, it takes everything within my being to walk a healthy path, despite all that I have gone through.

So much has changed over the last several years. We have seen incredible improvements in relationships between Aboriginal and non-Aboriginal people. Overt racism has significantly decreased. There have been many initiatives in the spirit of truth and reconciliation. The spirit of truth and reconciliation is certainly alive. For example, my hometowns of Smithers and Telkwa have changed as there has been an incredible level of reconciliatory steps that have been achieved over the last several years. In fact, there is a common effort on behalf of most to achieve reconciliation in north-central British Columbia and beyond. There is so much hope! While we collectively strive for reconciliation, it is vital to continue to listen to and hear the many experiences of trauma, as so many of us are still healing. It is important to acknowledge the truth and to try to understand our experiences and how it has affected us. This is how we can collectively reach touchpoints of reconciliation.

In my own process of healing, I continue to cling to the ways of my ancestors. I strive to maintain a strong connection to my identity as a Wet'suwet'en woman to embrace my culture

and continue on the trails of my ancestors. I
have achieved various degrees of healing by
clinging to the ways of my ancestors and striving
for physical, spiritual, emotional, and mental
well-being. Some of my solutions have come
through walking/snowshoeing on *Niwh Yintah*,
participating in the *Balhats*, striving for strong
and positive relationships, using all available
resources to help heal, Aikido, cycling, going to
church, and trying to embrace all that is good
through my journey and leave the rest behind.

My soulmate, the man I married in 2002,
has supported, respected, loved, honoured,
and upheld me. Our marriage has been such
an amazing blessing as he walked with me as
I underwent so much turmoil and pain. He
supported me through my education, and even
though there were moments of tremendous
challenge, we navigated the hardships together.
In the Wet'suwet'en culture, the term *necidildes*
can apply to a spouse. *Necidildes* is when a family
member or spouse is given permission to access
and use territorial resources. John has been an
ideal *necidildes* as we walk on *Niwh Yintah* softly
and with the utmost respect. He has assisted
me in various ways when harvesting, hunting,
snaring, and fishing. He has been such an
amazing part of my journey of healing and hope.

Despite some of the harsher realities and tension-filled relations, it is also very important to acknowledge all the relationships and all those who have incredibly kind hearts and strive for the best for all of us. For example, there were some high school teachers who were absolutely outstanding in their support and encouragement and also some in the post-secondary realm who have been tremendously supportive, like Dr. Sarah Carter and Dr. Chad Thompson. In addition, some Aboriginal people in the post-secondary realm have stood so strong in the face of great challenges, including Marlene Erickson. There are so many kind-hearted people who have been so influential and instrumental in my journey. It is so important to acknowledge relationships that are life-giving.

As we move through the process of truth and reconciliation, it is vitally important for us to share our truths. For without truth, we can't achieve reconciliation. This is why I chose to share this story of my truth. This is only one experience among so many. The healing journey can be painful as we reach back through our lives and revisit the traumas, but once we move through, we can continue on the trails of the ancestors, one step at a time.

Reconciliation

"While we collectively strive for reconciliation, it is vital to continue to listen to and to hear the many experiences of trauma, as so many of us are still healing. It is important to acknowledge the truth and to try to understand our experiences and how it has affected us. This is how we can collectively reach touchpoints of reconciliation."
—Corinne George

Endnotes

1   There are alternative spellings for "Wet'suwet'en" and "Gitksan," but I chose to use these spellings. It is also important to note that I often spell Wet'suwet'en words phonetically as opposed to the linguistic spellings.

2   Italicized names followed by English names are Hereditary Chief names. I won't translate the names to respect the current name holders as the names have been passed on to successors.

3   The Wet'suwet'en hereditary system honours names passed on from time immemorial. Thus, multiple people in the same lineage can hold the same hereditary name (i.e., Naqua'ohn). Further, in the case of my great grandmother Christine Patsy-Tom, she was honoured with two names, one Wet'suwet'en Naquao'ohn and the other Gitksan Noxalay.

4   Wet'suwet'en village, also known as Hagwilget, outside of Hazelton, BC.

5   It is important to note here that I do not claim to speak on anyone's behalf. This is my truth and my own personal experiences.

6   Wet'suwet'en meaning "setting snares around the lake." This is where some of my maternal ancestors thrived.

7   According to the British Columbia Archives, "Pre-emption was a method of acquiring provincial Crown land by claiming it for settlement and agricultural purposes." British Columbia Archives, "British Columbia Archives Research Guide: Quick Guide to Pre-Emption and Homestead Records," September 2012, Royal BC Museum, https://royalbcmuseum.bc.ca/assets/Pre-emptions_homesteads_quick_guide.pdf, 1.

8   "Carrier" is the name that settlers use for Aboriginal people in north-central British Columbia. The name comes from a tradition when women carried the remains of their husbands on their backs for one year following their death. Through the last decades, each group such as "Wet'suwet'en" reclaimed identities and our original names but we often acknowledge the "Carrier" name and also use the term in these types of contexts.

9   Now called, "Dze L'K'ant Friendship Centre."

10 Sarah Carter, *Aboriginal People and Colonizers of Western Canada to 1900* (Toronto: University of Toronto Press, 1999), 31.

11 Reconciliation Canada, "Walk for Reconciliation 2013: Namwayut, We Are All One," Reconciliation Canada, https://reconciliationcanada.ca/walk-for-reconciliation-2013/.

12 Morihei Ueshiba, *The Art of Peace*, trans. John Stevens (Boston: Shambhala Publications, 2002).

About the Author

Corinne George is Wet'suwet'en from the Gidimt'en Clan (Bear Clan). Corinne has a Master of Arts in history from the University of Calgary, where she wrote her thesis, "Grassroots Activism of Aboriginal Women in Calgary and Edmonton, 1951–1985." With extensive experience in research, writing, and teaching, Corinne strives for Truth and Reconciliation in all aspects of her life and seeks to integrate various levels of the United Nations Declaration on the Rights of Indigenous Peoples into her work. In her spare time, her hobbies include hiking, snowshoeing, cycling, and Aikido—for which she has earned her Nidan. Corinne has spent many years living in both Alberta and British Columbia. Currently, she lives in C'iggiz, Gidimt'en, Wet'suwet'en territory and she is the Regional Principal of the College of the New Caledonia-Burns Lake Campus.